IMAGES OF ENGLAND

GREAT YARMOUTH
AND
GORLESTON PUBS

IMAGES OF ENGLAND

GREAT YARMOUTH
AND
GORLESTON PUBS

COLIN TOOKE

TEMPUS

Frontispiece: Burroughs wine and spirit business was bought by Lacon's in 1897, three years after this advertisement appeared. Burroughs Stores (see page 17) was owned by William Norton Burroughs and later Thomas Proctor Burroughs and stood in the Market Place on the site of the present Gallon Pot. Although owned by Lacon's, it traded under its original name until the building was destroyed by an air raid in 1943.

First published 2004

Tempus Publishing Limited
The Mill, Brimscombe Port,
Stroud, Gloucestershire, GL5 2QG
www.tempus-publishing.com

British Library Cataloguing in Publication Data.
A catalogue record for this book is available from the British Library.

ISBN 0 7524 3298 2

Typesetting and origination by Tempus Publishing Limited.
Printed in Great Britain.

Contents

Acknowledgements

Many of the images in this book come from my own collection but I have also had to call upon the good will of Peter Allard, John Audley, Peter Jones and Clive Manson to use material from their collections. Other photographs have been supplied by Harry Eastoe, Alec McEwen and Molly Stanley. The information about the various pubs is the result of several years' research and a valuable source of information was the archive of Messrs Whitbread & Co. held at the brewery, Chiswell Street, London, and their archivist at the time, Nick Redman. Unfortunately this archive has now been dispersed and is no longer available for researchers. Also invaluable was the collection of books, documents and newspaper cuttings held in the Great Yarmouth Library, the Norfolk Record Office and the old Norwich Central Library, Colman & Rye Collection, much of the latter lost in a disastrous fire. My wife Jan has, as always, been on hand to offer advice and encouragement, without which this book would not have reached completion.

Although Lacon's stopped brewing over thirty-five years ago, these wall plaques can still be seen built into the walls of many pubs in Yarmouth and Gorleston today. Lacon's name also lives on in the internal decorations of many present-day pubs, on clocks and etched into mirrors and windows.

Introduction

There is nothing which has yet been contrived by man by which so much happiness is produced as by a good tavern or inn.
– Dr Johnson, eighteenth century.

The British public house has no counterpart anywhere else in the world. Other countries have tried to copy the idea but the 'pubs' of this country are today, and have always been, unique institutions. The public house or beerhouse of yesteryear played a somewhat different role in society than today's pub. Although today we usually make little distinction between different types of licensed premises and generally refer to them all as pubs, they were originally very different types of establishments. The inn, which first appeared in England in the fourteenth century when it was chiefly intended to provide food and rest for pilgrims, soon became a kind of institution where any traveller knew he could find accommodation and his horses could be stabled or changed. This was important in the days when the only way to travel any distance was on horseback or by stagecoach. Some of today's public houses still retain features of that period, in particular the Dukes Head on Hall Quay and the White Horse Inn at the northern end of the town. In both cases the entrance to the inn yard and the protective iron kerbs still exist.

A good inn had a staff of servants under a cheerful landlord, the chamberlain or chambermaid to show the traveller to his quarters, and the ostler to take care of the horses. There was no bar as we know it today and drinks were brought in on trays by serving wenches or lads. The inns were also known for the good, homely food that was always available. Today hotels have taken the place of inns.

The tavern did not provide accommodation like the inn and was the forerunner of the music hall. Before the days of music licences, many taverns utilised a large room, often equipped with a stage, for concerts and other entertainment. The Angel in the Market Place was renowned for this type of entertainment, as was the

Half Moon, the Bull and several other town-centre taverns. The tavern was allowed to sell beer and wine to all sections of the public whereas the inn was restricted to sales to residents only.

Ale houses or beerhouses, sometimes referred to as tippling houses, were private houses where beer was brewed in the kitchen and often retailed in the front room. In 1586 the number of tippling houses in Yarmouth was restricted to sixteen, a figure which had increased to 120 by 1705. In 1553 beer sold in Yarmouth at 3s 4d per thirty-two gallons. At this period, beer was being consumed in large quantities by men, women and children alike. Tea, coffee, chocolate and soft drinks were unknown and milk was only used for making butter and cheese. Water was not usually fit for drinking and therefore beer had to provide the necessary liquid intake for most people.

Many laws were introduced to try and control beerhouses. Gambling was officially prohibited and in Yarmouth in 1552 it was decreed that anyone caught smoking in a beerhouse was to be taken into custody. In 1591 it was decreed that 'a beerhouse or tavern could only be kept by a Freeman of the town, or the widow of a Freeman'. In 1711 the town ruled that no licence was to be granted to anyone to draw or retail ale or any other liquor at any house by the seaside except during the fishing season. In 1830 an Act of Parliament known as the 'Duke of Wellington's Beer House Act' was passed to ease the restrictions on the sale of ale and beer in an effort to discourage the growing consumption of spirits. In practice the Act only encouraged more disorderly places to open, for on payment of a two-guinea licence fee anyone could open a beerhouse. In 1834 there were 135 public houses and twenty-three beerhouses in Yarmouth and in 1841 the 'Sabbath Observance Society' reported that 144 shops in the town and 150 public houses (a figure which included beerhouses) were open on Sundays. This was a period of great expansion for the town as development spread across the Denes and waste ground towards the sea and by 1854 the number of public houses had risen to 184 with fifty beerhouses. As would be expected, the greatest concentration of pubs was found within the area of the old town, where there was often a licensed house on the corner of each row.

There were few restrictions on opening hours at this period, although in 1872 drinking time was cut to seventeen hours a day, the taverns opening at 6.00 a.m. and closing at 11.00 p.m. In 1915 opening hours were restricted during the afternoon period, an attempt to curtail the drinking habits of the munitions workers, some of whom spent more time drinking than they did working. The Prime Minister of the day, Lloyd George, is quoted as saying, 'drink is doing more damage than all the German submarines put together'. It was to be seventy-three years before opening hours were extended again, on 22 August 1988, when a new Act came into force allowing licensed premises to open from 11.00 a.m. to 11.00 p.m.

By the end of the eighteenth century it was normal for the publican to pay the brewery at the end of each month on sales, not deliveries. The collecting clerk called each month to check sales and the remaining stock, taking payment from the publican only for the sales of the month. A publican could also return to the brewery any unsold beer, or beer in poor condition. In August 1852 the Gt Yarmouth Licensed Victuallers Protection Society was formed at a meeting held at the St George's Tavern, King Street. The objects of the society were to 'protect the trade from Beer Houses who open outside the hours allowed by the current regulations and to prevent a licence being granted to any property below a stipulated rateable value'. Members were also protected against loss of trade through 'robbery by servants, stealing of pots and every kind of theft'. In January 1873 the name of the organisation was changed to the Gt Yarmouth Licensed Victuallers Association.

This was also a period when the Temperance movement was strong in many parts of the country, although Great Yarmouth does not seem to have been one of their most successful strongholds. In 1858 the annual meeting of the local Temperance Society reported a disappointing year, making little progress at their thirty-one public meetings. Despite the claim that drinks 'are the means of damning more souls than all the ministers of the gospel are instrumental in saving' the inhabitants of the town took little notice. Indeed at one meeting the Revd Thomas Atkins had to cut short his lecture in the face of much opposition and he was 'in a most contemptible minority'. No doubt the large seafaring population of the town contributed to this hostility towards the Temperance movement. In 1891 Tom Goate opened the Cromwell Temperance Hotel on Hall Quay, a building that in later years was to become the present Star Hotel. This remained one of the town's premier temperance hotels until 1930.

In 1903 the councillors toured every licensed house in the town, the number of premises visited in Yarmouth and Gorleston totalling 258. By 1908 the number of licensed houses in the town was 295 but this figure included Grocer's licences and at that time was equal to one licensed property for every 180 persons.

In nineteenth-century elections only Freemen, and later householders with an annual rent of over £10, were allowed to vote. Bribery and corruption were rife and the pub played a key role in this dubious form of electioneering. The number of voters registered in the town in 1865 was 1,647 and as an inducement to vote free beer was provided by the respective parties, in addition to payments for loss of time from work and the customary payment or bribe for the actual vote. At the 1831 elections the Blue party paid out a total of £400 in tavern bills. The Apollo Gardens submitted a bill for £27 5s 4d to the Whig party, while the Kings Arms in Northgate Street supplied beer to the value of £10 15s. The public house was also the platform from where the parties addressed their followers. From the balcony of the Angel the Tory party candidate made his speeches to large crowds gathered in the Market Place, while the Whigs were doing the same from the balcony of the Crown & Anchor on Hall Quay.

As might be expected in a seafaring town like Yarmouth, there had always been a problem with disorderly houses. An enquiry of 1834 looked into the problem and came to the conclusion that much of the blame lay on the brewers themselves. When one tenant complained that he could not make a living at his house he was told by the brewery to 'get a lot of girls and a fiddler and you will do plenty of business'. The enquiry found that the brewers encouraged 'all sorts of evil company' and that 'the principal of injustice, injurious to the morals of the people, had pervaded the Licensing system'. It is interesting to note that two principal brewers in the town, Reynolds and Mortlock Lacon were both magistrates and sat on the Licensing Committee. A local grocer gave to an enquiry an example of the problems that arose. He quoted the case of the Humber Keel, previously known as the Duncan's Head. This had been closed at the same time as the Globe, where the landlady had her licence suspended for running a disorderly house. When the licensing came round again the following September, this same lady was given the licence of the Humber Keel, which reopened. The house then became even more disorderly than before and 'a great nuisance to the neighbourhood, the opening times extended to midnight'.

Prior to 1904 the justices could only remove a licence for cases of misconduct, but the Licensing Act of that year included a clause that enabled public houses 'surplus to requirements' to be closed and established the principle whereby owners were compensated for the loss of a licence. The money for compensation payments was raised from a levy on other licensed premises and between 1905 and 1914 many licences were withdrawn in the town.

In the period before the Second World War, Lacon's owned 180 public houses in the area of Yarmouth, 120 in the town itself, twenty-three in Southtown and Gorleston and another thirty-seven in the country villages. The war took its toll; twenty-two houses were closed in 1940 and another eighteen in 1941, many to never reopen. Bombing, particularly in the Middlegate area, destroyed several pubs, and post-war Yarmouth saw a great reduction in the number of licensed houses compared with the turn of the century. In 1946 the first darts league in the town was started in the Steward & Patteson pubs, followed the next year by a similar league in the Lacon's pubs.

The second half of the twentieth century saw a lot of change in the licensed trade. Local breweries were absorbed by the large national concerns and public houses changed ownership with ever-increasing frequency. Drinking habits also changed; mild beer sales declined sharply, while the lighter lager beers increased in popularity. Pressurised casks were introduced, something the old beerhouse keeper would not have considered possible when all beer was drawn 'straight from the wood'. Since the beginning of the eighteenth century there has been, at different times, almost 400 beerhouses, pubs, inns and taverns in Great Yarmouth and Gorleston. Today public houses frequently change name, landlord or tenant and brewery, and at the time this book was compiled there were 117 pubs open in Great Yarmouth and Gorleston. This figure excludes hotels and other premises with licensed bars.

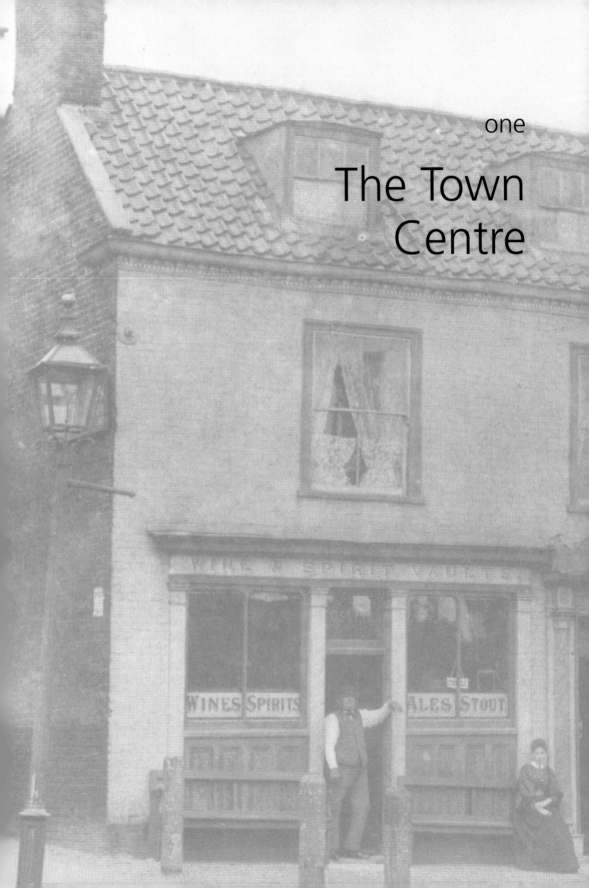

one

The Town
Centre

The first chapter of this book looks at some of the pubs in the town centre, around the market, and extending northwards along Northgate Street and Caister Road and southwards along King Street to Friars Lane. The Market Place is an area that has been the focal point of the town and centre of business for hundreds of years. From the Market Cross (the last of which was demolished in 1836) all-important announcements were made, while the stocks and pillory served out punishment to dishonest traders such as brewers for producing bad beer. Fairs have been held in the Market Place from 1638, important occasions for traders as well as merrymakers. The Market Place has also been the scene for great public rejoicing, including firework displays and bullock roasting. At either end of the Market are the 'Plains', Theatre, Priory and Church. These were originally designed as open areas where the market traders could unload and leave their carts on market days, stabling their horses at nearby inns such as the Feathers and the White Horse. This area of the town required its fair share of inns, taverns and pubs to satisfy the diverse needs of the merchants, traders and revellers. Also in the centre of the town was the brewery of E. Lacon & Co., Yarmouth brewers for over 200 years until closure in 1968. Lacon's Falcon Brewery produced the brew for at least half the pubs in the town, competing with the Norwich Brewery of Steward & Patteson. Although the town had many small brewers up to the middle of the nineteenth century, Lacon's and Steward & Patteson had become the dominant suppliers to local pubs by 1900.

At one time Northgate Street and Caister Road formed the main coaching route into the town, indeed it was the only route where it was possible to enter the town without crossing a river. Along this road were to be found the many inns and taverns serving the needs of travellers, such as the Kings Arms and the White Horse. Smaller pubs, such as the Coach & Horses, the East & West Flegg and the Jolly Farmers, served the market folk bringing their produce to the town's twice-weekly market.

In a southerly direction, King Street was not only one of the main shopping streets in the town but also a street with a large number of pubs. These included the Old White Lion and Liberty's, which are still trading, and others such as the Humber Keel and the Shakespeare, which have long since closed. The name King Street dates from the seventeenth century, when Charles II visited the town and, finding the town much to his liking, said he did not think he had such a place in his dominions. In recent years King Street has become a centre for nightlife, with many licensed premises such as Peggotty's and Red Square opening until the early hours.

Lacon's Brewery, Church Plain. A brewery had stood on this site for almost 300 years, but it closed in 1968 after being taken over by Whitbread's, making 150 employees redundant. The buildings were demolished in 1973 and a new Tesco store opened on the site in 1980, but this closed in 2002.

A delivery lorry outside the brewery in the 1960s. In the nineteenth century Lacon's used Troll Carts to deliver beer to local houses and steam wagons for those further afield. A Troll Cart was a narrow horse-drawn vehicle unique to Yarmouth in the eighteenth and nineteenth centuries. Used to negotiate the narrow Rows, it was not found in any other part of the country.

Opposite above: The Edinburgh was earlier known as the Half Moon, on the corner of Row 29. Robert Giles was landlord in 1868. This was a Lacon's pub which closed in 1922 and today the Red Cross charity shop stands on the site.

Left: The Market Distillery, seen here in the 1950s, was also well known as the Red House, famous for the model railway that ran round the bar at picture rail height. The railway had been installed by Teddy Moore, landlord until 1952. When the pub closed in 1961 it became part of Palmers department store until the site was redeveloped in the 1970s.

Below: When this picture was taken around 1880, it was known as the Elephant & Castle. This was a Steward & Patteson house and the name changed to the Distillery in 1904. The pub, between Rows 56 and 58, had a large concert room where entertainment was held every evening.

The Angel Hotel was one of the town's oldest inns, established by 1652, and one of the principal coaching inns of the nineteenth century. The licence was removed in 1939 and throughout the war years was used as a British Restaurant. The building was demolished in 1957 and today two shops stand on the site, Dixons and a building society.

Row 24, on the right in the picture, is today the southern pavement of the Conge. Foulshams Dining Rooms, seen here in 1899, had been bought by Lacon's in 1894, the spirit stores were licensed as the Blue Anchor. Following the closure of the dining rooms the pub remained until 1964 when it was demolished and today the NatWest bank stands on this corner site.

Burroughs' Stores,
1 & 2 Market Place,
Gt. Yarmouth
The Oldest
Licensed House
in the Distric

Burroughs Stores at Nos 1 and 2 Market Place, on the corner with Church Plain, was destroyed by an air raid in 1943. It was first licensed in 1772 by Richard Brighten, a brewer, and taken over by the Burroughs family in 1812. The building was rebuilt in 1959 and today is the Gallon Pot.

The Bull Hotel on the corner of Market Gates was a large pub with a separate concert room. Before 1819 it had been owned by Bells Gorleston brewery and was known as the British Hero. The licence was removed in 1911 and it then became the corn store of Arthur Hollis for many years. The lines across the picture are tram wires and electricity wires. John Keeble was landlord from 1896 until 1904.

Above: Fish Stall House had originally been known as the Jolly Butchers and then the Market Tavern. This part of the market had until 1869 been the fish market and Fish Street ran behind the property. This picture was taken in July 1907, but what the interested group has gathered around in the market is unknown. Beside the pub is one of the many bazaars to be found in the town at that time and to the right of that can be seen the old Theatre Royal in Theatre Plain, advertising a play entitled *The Superior Miss Pellender*. The pub and adjacent buildings were demolished in 1972 to make way for the new Market Gates shopping precinct.

Opposite above: The Feathers in Market Gates is probably the oldest pub in the town. The original building was recorded as a licensed house in 1581 and the Court of Charles II were entertained here in 1672. The room on the right of the entrance was the 'market room', popular on market days with country traders who had stabled their horses at the Feathers.

Opposite below: This 1890s view of Fullers Hill shows the Crystal, then known as the Captain Harmer, on the right and in the distance the Albion, earlier known as the Sawyers Arms. In the group of buildings on the left is the Jolly Waterman, on the corner with George Street. The Jolly Waterman closed in 1903, the Albion in 1913, and the Crystal remains open today.

White Horse Plain in 1957. It must have been just after Easter when the annual fair occupied the Market Place and the market stalls would seek temporary sites on the Plains, such as here. Behind the stalls can be seen the glass roof of the underground toilets, removed several years ago. In the background is the White Horse Inn, one of the town's oldest coaching inns and the starting point for many carriers carts which ran a regular service to outlying villages. The entrance to the yard, where there was accommodation for eighteen horses, still survives today. In front of the pub was a public weighbridge first installed in 1885 but now unused for many years. The shop of Henry Nichols, to the left of the White Horse, was at one time the Yew Tree pub, a name later changed to the Fishermans and Shrimpers Arms, closed in 1904.

Opposite above: Lacon's maltings in Rampart Road in 1971. These extensive malting were first built in 1705, rebuilt in 1912 and again in 1949 and demolished in 1972 when a telephone exchange was built on the site. Lacon's owned maltings in many parts of the town in the nineteenth century. The White Swan pub can be seen just past the maltings.

Opposite below: The Saracens Head, originally the Cart & Horse, on the corner of Church Plain and Northgate Street. Closed in 1970, it is today an insurance office.

Above: On the corner of Garrison Walk, now Garrison Road, stood the Waggon & Horses, a pub which had taken its licence from an ancient half-timbered pub on the opposite side of the road known as the Glass & Bottle. In 1819 the Waggon & Horses was owned by Paget's Brewery but eventually became a Lacon's pub before it closed in August 1905. Carriers carts left here for the villages of Thurne, Winterton and Stokesby. Gosling was landlord from 1892 until 1896. Shortly after it closed the building was demolished and the licence was transferred to the new Lacon Arms on Alderson Road.

Opposite above: The old Kings Arms in Northgate Street, seen here in September 1880, extended as far as the churchyard. On the front of the building is a steelyard, an early device for weighing wagons before the weighbridge was invented. The Kings Arms was rebuilt early in the twentieth century.

Opposite below: The East & West Flegg, a Lacon's pub which closed in 1925, was on the corner of Row 2. It had earlier been called the Bird in Hand and the Black Horse. This pub had stables for twenty-seven horses, used on market days together with a designated room for the market traders who travelled in from the villages each Wednesday and Saturday.

The Queen Victoria, a small beerhouse in Northgate Street, opened in the 1860s and closed in 1931 when the licence was transferred to the rebuilt Apollo Tavern on the opposite side of the road. The property is now a butcher's shop. The Artis family were licensees for over forty-five years until 1919. It was the headquarters of the Yarmouth Artesians Golf Club.

The Nursery Tavern opened in 1872 built on land that had previously been nursery gardens. It was bought by Lacon's in 1912 and reconstructed in 1922. This picture was taken in the late 1920s. The pub closed in 1958 and for many years has been Weldon's fruit and vegetable shop.

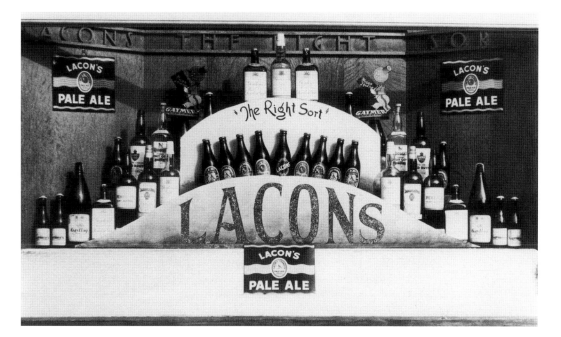

Above: A window display of Lacon's beers and spirits.

Right: The Rose in King Street closed in 1906. It was separated from Divers by a shop and was another pub that extended through to Theatre Plain, having an entrance at either end. The tram wires in this picture indicate it was taken between 1902 and 1906 when A.D. Aldridge was landlord.

Above: For many years the Regent Road/King Street corner was known as Divers Corner. Here was a large public house called the Old Gallon Pot but always known as Divers. The building seen here was erected in 1856 but partly demolished in the 1920s to allow Regent Road to be widened.

Left: Divers extended through to Theatre Plain, seen here in the 1970s. The pub closed in February 1974 and was demolished a few years later to be replaced by new shops.

Opposite above: The Penrice Arms and next door the Jamaica Stores or Old Jamaica Rum Stores. The Penrice took its name from Thomas Penrice who had a coach house on the site in the seventeenth century. The Jamacia closed in 1931 and for many years was the fish shop of Cubitt & Sons.

The Penrice Arms changed to the One-Five-One club in December 1978, retaining its old Lacon's clock and mirror as part of the 1970s décor. Seated at the bar is the then owner of the new club, Peter Jay.

The Old White Lion in King Street is seen here when Thomas Crome was licensee, *c.* 1930. This is one of the oldest licensed houses in the town, dating from the seventeenth century. Row 130 can be seen on the right, today this is the pavement of Nottingham Way.

The Brunswick Hotel opened in 1886 as a Temperance hotel. It later became a leading Commercial Hotel catering for travelling representatives. A family of holidaymakers has just arrived in the hotel's station fly, which was sent to meet each incoming train. Walter Bliss owned the Brunswick from 1907 until 1946.

Left: On the corner of Row 140 was the Earl St Vincent. A small Lacon's pub, it was badly damaged in the Second World War and demolished in 1949. Earl St Vincent was a title given to John Jarvis, one of the town's popular naval heroes who defeated a Spanish fleet in 1797 and was subsequently made a Freeman of the town.

Below: From 1907 until 1927 the landlord of the Earl St Vincent in King Street was Robert Edwards, seen here behind the bar with his wife, *c.* 1920.

Above: Four breweries, Reynolds, Harpers, Ferriers and Steward & Patteson, before Lacon's had owned the Lion and Lamb, on the corner of Row 109. In 1987 the name changed to Manhattans and a year later to Kitty Witches, a name taken from Row 95 further along King Street. In the 1980s it changed to its present name, Liberty's, a pub with an American rock café theme.

Left: On the corner of Regent Street and King Street stood the Crown until it was demolished in 1967 and a shop built on the site. The Crown is the most popular pub name in the country.

two

The
Old Town

PERS
WASHES W

HEI

57

The old town within the medieval town walls was made up by the 145 Rows which ran east to west and three narrow streets, Howard Street, George Street and Middlegate which ran north to south. For 800 years the whole population of the town lived within this somewhat confined area. The rows contained both large and small dwelling houses, while along the streets were to be found the shops, pubs and other commercial premises. In many instances a pub was to be found on the corner of almost every row and many rows took their names from the corner pub. Very few of these pubs remain today as post-war redevelopment replaced most of the old town with new housing and new streets. In 1890 Lacon's purchased and demolished a lot of property in George Street to expand the brewery, one casualty of this being the Grapes. In 1886 there were thirteen pubs in George Street, a figure that had reduced to six by 1911 and just one today, the Mitre. Among the pubs now gone are the Wheel of Fortune, first recorded in 1742, and the Griffin, on the corner of Row 45, burnt down in 1914.

There have been a total of thirty-two pubs in Howard Street over the years, including some which had a very dubious reputation. These included the Globe, closed as a disreputable house in 1861, and the Prince of Wales. The most notorious of all was the Victoria, on the corner of Row 26, which had a basement drinking den known as Hell's Hole. This was a favourite haunt for foreign sailors and it eventually lost its licence in 1880. O'Grady's, in Howard Street, is a modern name for a pub which has changed its name twelve times, eight of these changes taking place since 1990.

Middlegate Street, for many years known as Gaol Street because of the Tolhouse Gaol, had twenty-four pubs in 1863, a figure reduced to twenty by 1886 and ten by 1938. Today, after post-war redevelopment, only two, the Ship and Allen's, remain. In Row 113, which led off Middlegate, was the Bee, one of the few pubs which was to be found in a row. As with Howard Street, there were many pubs in Middlegate with a bad reputation, one of which was the Sailors Return. In 1819 the Tuns Inn was sold to the Corporation, to be demolished to make way for an extension to the gaol. In 1735 a murder took place at the Tuns; the landlady was tried, found guilty and hanged. Many years later a man confessed to being the real murderer in a death-bed confession. Another murder in Middlegate occurred in 1934 when Horace Butcher was found dead in his shop by the landlord of the next door Druids Arms (see page 33). This remains one of the town's unsolved murders.

The Druids Arms,
150 Middlegate St.,
Gt. Yarmouth.
E. Aldous Proprietor

Above: The Druids Arms, at 150 Middlegate Street and on the corner of Row 117, was owned by the Clochester Brewery Co. before Lacon's took it over.

Right: The landlord in the 1930s was Edgar Aldous, seen here in the doorway. Next door was the shop of Horace Butcher, a rag and bone merchant who was found murdered in his shop in 1934. It was Edgar Aldous who found Horace with his head battered and the murder weapon, a 7lb weight with blood and hair on it, lying beside the body. To this day the crime remains unsolved.

One of the oldest and smallest pubs in Middlegate was the Cock, seen here in a street scene of the early 1870s. By 1874 the Cock had been rebuilt and renamed the Middlegate Tavern, a Lacon pub which finally closed in 1940. Many of the buildings seen in this picture date from the seventeenth century and Cock Alley ran from King Street to the rear of the pub.

Above: A view of Middlegate, painted by
C.H. Harrison in 1895, showing the
rebuilt Middlegate Tavern on the left.
The date letters 1682 on the adjacent
building show how ancient some of the
property in the street was. On the right is
the entrance to Row 140 and part of the
Liverpool Tavern.

Right: The Middlegate Tavern in the
1920s. The old buildings adjoining it, seen
in the above painting, have been
demolished and the Co-op fish-canning
factory has opened.

On the corner of Row 139 was the Magdala Tavern, a pub that had been rebuilt in 1897. It is seen here in the 1930s when Henry George King was landlord. Like most of Middlegate Street this property was demolished in the 1950s post-war redevelopment of the area.

On the corner of Row 142 was the Fishing Boat, 111 Middlegate Street, a Lacon pub which closed in 1938 when William Godbolt was landlord.

Above: The western side of Middlegate Street looking south from Friars Lane. In the centre of the picture can be seen Row 145, the last row, and on the corner the Fourteen Stars, which was later renamed the Nottingham Arms. This pub lost its licence in 1890.

Left: A wartime picture showing the property of Delf & Sons at 67 Middlegate Street, which had been the Tomlinson Arms until 1904. The old pub façade was retained by the new business. The gate across the road marks the boundary of the military controlled area of Middlegate that throughout 1942 was used as a training ground for close combat fighting.

These two pictures show Lacon's entries in the Great Yarmouth Carnivals. The car is decorated for the 1924 carnival, while the horse dray outside the brewery is ready for the 1934 carnival procession, ten years later. These carnivals were week-long events, most of the local businesses taking part.

Above: Middlegate Street with the ancient Tolhouse on the left, now a museum. On the opposite side of the road the man is standing outside the Tolhouse Tavern on the corner of Row 107, St Georges Row East. Almost all the property in this picture except the Tolhouse and Salvation Army building was demolished in the post-war redevelopment.

Right: The Tolhouse Tavern with the landlord Joseph William Coney standing in the doorway, *c.* 1930. This was a Lacon's pub and closed in June 1933. Before 1895 it had been known as the Welcome Sailor, an eating house as well as a beerhouse.

The Suffolk Tavern, 166 Middlegate Street, was a Lacon's pub which closed in 1942 due to bomb damage but was repaired and reopened after the war. The licence was finally removed in 1950 when it was demolished. Adjoining the pub to the south was the Salvation Army Hall that today is one of the few buildings still remaining of the original Middlegate.

At the southern end of Middlegate Street, on the corner with Friars Lane, was the Yarmouth Fishery. This small Lacon's pub closed in 1938 after being kept for three generations by the Tripp family.

BARNBY & SON,

DIRECT IMPORTERS OF

WINES, SPIRITS,

AND

LIQUERS,

38, CHARLOTTE STREET

GREAT YARMOUTH.

SOLE AGENTS FOR

ELLIOT, WATNEY, AND CO.'S

London Stout, Porter, &c.

AITCHISONS EDINBURGH STRONG ALES,

Bass & Co.'s East India Pale Ales,

WORTHINGTON'S STRONG BURTON & PALE ALES,

GUINNESS & CO.'S EXTRA DOUBLE STOUT,

PEMARTIN & CO'S SHERRIES,

Geo. G. Sandeman, Sons, & Co.'s Ports,

ETC., ETC., ETC.

PRICE LIST FREE UPON APPLICATION.

Carriage paid on Wines and Spirits to any distance, by one direct Conveyance.

In the nineteenth century Barnby Wine Stores was at 38 Charlotte Street, a street that was renamed Howard Street North. The wine stores were bought by Lacon's and became the Gallon Pot.

The Gallon Pot (earlier Barnby Wine Stores) on the corner of Row 42 was a Lacon's pub that was demolished in 1956 when the area was cleared for post-war housing development. In 1930 this was one of the pubs granted a music licence 'for wireless only'.

The New Queens Head was on the corner of Row 50 that today forms the northern pavement of Stonecutters Way. The pub closed in 1926, the site now an open space on the corner of Broad Row.

Left: Behind the Dukes Head Hotel was the Corn Exchange in Howard Street. Part of the Corn Exchange was a pub known as the Exchange Vaults, a Lacon's pub that closed in 1939. Until 1953 the building was used as the HQ of the RAFA Roundel Club. It was demolished in 1956.

Opposite: A beer delivery at an unknown location by one of Lacon's Clayton Steam Wagons. These vehicles usually made deliveries to out of town pubs, the horse-drawn drays and Troll Carts being used within the town.

The old Burton Arms in Howard Street was demolished in 1959, the present pub of that name standing on the same site. The original beerhouse had been known as the Lancer, later changed to the Colchester and then the Edward VII. It was named the Burton Arms in 1935.

Between Rows 57 and 59 is a pub that has changed its name more times than any other pub in the town. There has been a pub on this site since at least 1761 and by 1891 it was known as the Carpenters Arms. It is now O'Grady's but in between there have been ten other names. It was the Silver Herring from 1969 until 1977.

Right: Labels from Lacon's Audit Ales. When the brewhouses at the Oxford and Cambridge colleges closed, larger breweries such as Lacon's took over. From 1923 Lacon's brewed this special ale for some Cambridge colleges and bottled it in champagne quarts with special labels. The brew was also available in local pubs.

Opposite below: For the first half of the twentieth century S.J. Allen were wine and spirit merchants at No. 28 Howard Street. This had previously been a pub known as the City of London Tavern, which had a large concert room. From 1956 it was the Talbot Wine Vaults and today it is the Talbot. The name comes from a large breed of hunting dog, white with black spots, popular in the Middle Ages but now extinct in its true form.

The Mariners Tavern, No. 69 Howard Street, was originally called the Three Jolly Mariners but by 1850 had changed to the name it retains today. It was rebuilt after the war in the distinctive 'Lacon style' of architecture, designed by E.W. Ecclestone, reopening in March 1951.

At No. 29 Howard Street South was the Enterprise, on the corner of Row 80. This was originally a beerhouse known as the Three Pigeons, later changed to the Lobster. By 1819 it was the Jolly Maltsters and by 1874 the Enterprise. It closed in 1952.

Right: Howard Street South in the 1920s looking towards Regent Street. The end of the Arcade is behind the man standing in the road. Over the years there have been thirty-two licensed premises in Howard Street, some of them the most notorious and disreputable in the town.

Below: A vehicle used in the London area to deliver Lacon's beers. This one is on hire from a contractor, Charles Wells of East London. Note the solid tyres. Lacon's owned twenty-seven pubs in London and had stores and stables in Bethnal Green.

Right: George Street looking from Fullers Hill in 1939.

Below: The Wheel of Fortune, on the corner of Row 30 in George Street, had been a beerhouse for over 200 years. It was named in documents dated 1742, when John Thacker was hanged on the Denes for killing John Auger with a pistol ball 'in a shop near the Wheel of Fortune'. The pub closed in 1938.

three

Along the Riverside

FOLK BEERS BREWED FROM ENGLISH BARLEY.

North Quay, Hall Quay and South Quay make up the riverside area of the town and, as would be expected, had their fair share of pubs, particularly in the nineteenth century. North Quay was also the site of one of the town's early breweries, that of Paget & Co. Established in 1734 this brewery finally closed in 1847 when the site was bought by the railway company to make the approach for their new bridge across the river, connecting to the recently opened Vauxhall Station. With the opening of the railway in 1844, three pubs along this part of the quay changed their names in an attempt to attract custom from rail travellers. The Dolphin changed to the Railway Terminus, The Falcon to the Excursion Train Tavern and the Quay Mill to the Railway Tavern. At the southern end of the quay was the distribution depot of Steward & Patteson, the Norwich brewers, and also one of their pubs, the Cellar House. Beer from Norwich was bottled here until 1969 when the site was sold and the present Havenbridge House erected.

Hall Quay, the centre of the riverside area, has always been an important banking and commercial area. Between the banks are some large pubs including the Dukes Head, originally an Elizabethan merchant's house dating from 1609. This was also one of the town's coaching inns, the London stagecoach leaving here three times a week at 5.00 a.m. and, after an overnight stop at Ipswich, arriving in London the following evening at 7.00 p.m. The present HSBC bank was built as the Yare Hotel in 1938 on the site of two earlier pubs, the Steam Packet and the Crown & Anchor. The present Star Hotel, another Elizabethan building, was the Cromwell Temperance Hotel from 1890. The original Star was demolished in 1930 to make way for a telephone exchange, the name and licence being transferred to the Cromwell.

South Quay, between the Town Hall and Friars Lane, was at one time the home of many of the town's merchants. Their large impressive houses were interspersed with small pubs as this was the main working part of the quay, an area of great activity. The town's only floating pub, the Celtic Surveyor, was moored here in 1983, a short-lived venture which was eventually arrested for non-payment of harbour dues. Not many pubs can say they went out of business because they were arrested. Many pub names along this part of the quay had maritime-related names such as the Ballast Keel, Ferry Hotel, Mariners Compass and the present-day Quayside Tavern. Further south, close to the shipbuilding yards of the nineteenth century, were the Wet Dock Tavern, Jolly Chaulkers and Ship on the Stocks. The Greenland Whale Fishery reflected the days when the town took part in whale fishing off Spitzbergen and Greenland.

To the left of the old suspension bridge across the River Bure can be seen the dance hall of the Vauxhall Pleasure Gardens, here called the 'Dramatic Saloon'. Today this is the site of the Car Wash opposite the station forecourt. Pleasure gardens were an important part of Victorian social life, providing entertainment as well as food and drink.

The railway station was built on part of the Vauxhall Gardens in 1844. Opposite the station entrance were the Railway Refreshment Rooms that later became the Vauxhall Gardens pub. This pub, seen here in December 1974, closed in March 1989 and was demolished the following year.

The original White Swan dated from the eighteenth century but was rebuilt in the nineteenth century. It was owned by Paget's Brewery and later Steward & Pattesons. The White Swan was a popular pub with the wherrymen, many of whom lived in this part of the town.

The White Swan in May 1971, looking from the bridge as work began to realign the road to the east side of the pub. This work was combined with a new bridge over the river which opened the following year.

Above: Almost opposite the White Swan was the Lord Collingwood, seen here in 1906 two years after it had closed as a pub. From 1824 until 1870 the landlord had been John Bessey. This site is now the road in front of the Telephone Exchange, Laughing Image Corner.

Left: Between Rainbow Corner and Row 8 was the North Tower, a pub that closed in 1969. This is now the site of the post office on North Quay. Like many pubs in the town there was no cellar at the North Tower and beer was 'drawn straight from the wood'.

In the centre of this 1953 aerial picture is the church of St Andrews, now the site of Staples office warehouse, and to the south of that the extensive bottle store of Lacon's, now rebuilt as the Aldi supermarket. In the top left of the picture are the buildings of Lacon's Brewery. At the bottom of the picture is one of the many Lacon's malthouses that were to be found in the town. On the corner of Fullers Hill is a house, which until 1933 had been the North Star pub. Almost all the buildings seen in this picture have now been demolished.

North Quay in the 1950s. In the row of buildings seen here were three pubs, the Norwich Arms on the left (closed 1904), the North Tower (closed 1969) and at the far end the North Star (closed 1933). In the background is the brewery chimney.

The foundation stone of the new Brewery Stores on North Quay was laid on 15 June 1895 by Mrs Ernest de Montesque Lacon, wife of the chairman of the directors. The building was badly damaged by enemy action on 25 June 1942 and rebuilt in 1948.

Left: A rail line ran into the Brewery Stores and from here beer was sent to London in special wagons bearing the Lacon name. The line connected with the quayside tramway and then Vauxhall station. The railway staff are seen here in the 1890s.

Below: Workers at the Brewery Stores in the 1890s. No doubt the man on the right is the foreman, but the other workers appear to be quite young.

The Brewery Stores in 1988 after Whitbread's had decided the building was surplus to requirements and local pubs would be served from distribution depots further afield. The building was demolished and the present Aldi store built on the site.

The decorative tiled panel on the North Quay Brewery Stores showing the Lacon falcon. Unfortunately this tiled panel was destroyed during the demolition work.

Opposite above: The Railway Tavern on North Quay was on the corner of the Conge. William Holland was landlord from 1920 until 1928. The pub had earlier been known as the Dolphin and the Railway Terminus. In the 1930s the landlord was Albert Mummery, a well-known local footballer. The pub closed in 1937 and in 1948 Johnson's clothing factory was built on the site.

Opposite below: This all-male gathering suggests a pub outing from the Royal George on North Quay in the early twentieth century. The four-horse brake would have taken the party as far as Ormesby, California or Belton Gardens for their day out. No doubt a few crates of beer are stored under the seats.

Right, above: The Quay Mill on North Quay was earlier called the Hunter Cutter, the Windmill and, in the nineteenth century, the Railway Tavern. One room in the Quay Mill was designated the 'Bagatelle Room', a predecessor of the pool table. The pub closed in 1941 and now the Kingdom Hall of the Jehovah's Witnesses stands on the site.

Right: The bar in the Quay Mill, probably in the late 1920s. The pub took its name from an early windmill which stood opposite, on the riverbank, demolished in 1799.

Until 1969 this building was the office of Steward & Patteson. The company had purchased the private house in 1908 and converted it into their offices. After being sold in 1972, the house was demolished and the office block known as Havenbridge House was built on the site.

Although Steward & Patteson did not have a brewery in the town, they had extensive stores and distribution facilities on North Quay, seen here in April 1902. From here beer was delivered to over 100 outlets. By 1936 there was a staff of twenty-seven men, which included ten draymen and six bottle boys. On the right in the picture is the Cellar House pub.

The Steward & Patteson steam wherry *Annie* which, until 1939, brought two loads from the Norwich Brewery each week in winter and three loads each week in summer. Each load consisted of forty tons of beer, the barrels in the hold and, as can be seen here, the bottled beer on the deck.

Beer being loaded at the North Quay depot in the early 1950s. The company had phased out the horse drays at the beginning of the Second World War and replaced them with five lorries.

The Buck Inn, Hall Quay, closed in 1927 and public toilets and slipper baths were built on the site, now the corner of Stonecutters Way.

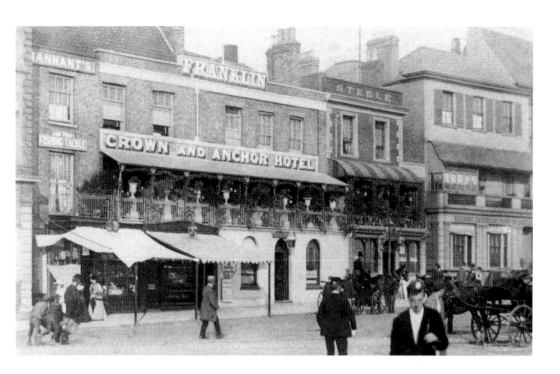

Above: The Crown & Anchor and the adjoining Steam Packet were demolished in 1938. At the Crown & Anchor the annual Sprat Banquet was held where white sprats, boiled sprats, cured sprats and sprats à la Mansion House were served. The Steam Packet was originally called the Coalmeters.

Right: This advertisement for the Steam Packet dates from 1886.

Opposite below: The Dukes Head in 1945. The building dates from 1609 and this was one of the main coaching inns in the town. Every Monday, Wednesday and Friday a stagecoach known as the Dukes Head coach left here at 5.00 a.m., arriving in Ipswich in the afternoon. After an overnight stop the coach arrived in London at 7.00 p.m. On the left is Henry's café, known to most people as the Greasy Spoon, but originally a pub called the Barge Tavern.

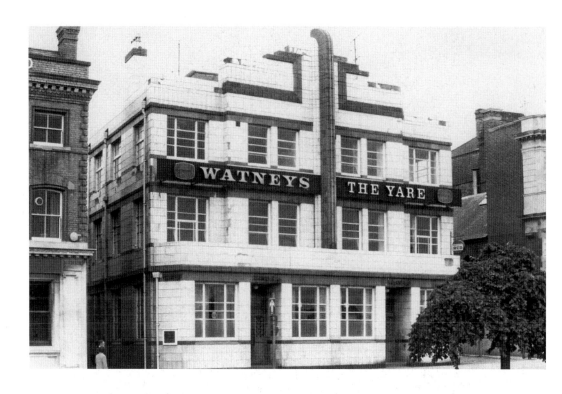

In the old Star were some fine plaster ceilings and panelled rooms including this one, which was known as the Nelson Room, and where a portrait of Nelson once hung over the fireplace. The panelling from this room was sold by auction in 1913 and is now displayed in the Metropolitan Museum, New York.

Opposite above: Following the demolition of the Crown & Anchor and the Steam Packet, the Yare Hotel rose on the site, opening in 1939. Seen here just before it closed in May 1974, the building was converted into the Midland Bank, now the HSBC, four years later.

Opposite below: The original Star Hotel with the station fly waiting outside. This fine Elizabethan building was bought in 1930 to be demolished and a telephone exchange built on the site. The licence was transferred to the adjacent Cromwell Hotel. This picture is from before 1890 as on the left is the two-story Stone House Hotel, later to become the Cromwell.

Above: The Cromwell Hotel when it was still a Temperance and Commercial Hotel, *c.* 1910. The upper floors had been added in 1890. The old Star Hotel can be seen on the right, both hotels having the luggage barrows ready. In 1930 the Cromwell was to change its name to become the Star.

Opposite below: This view of the South Quay in the nineteenth century shows some of the fine buildings which lined the quay at that time. The lamp post is outside the Newcastle Tavern which later changed its name to the Ferry Hotel, a Lacon's pub. It closed in 1941 and today this is the southern corner of Nottingham Way.

The town's only floating pub was the short-lived Celtic Surveyor, opened in 1983 and moored opposite the Town Hall. In 1984 the ship was arrested by the Port & Haven Commissioners for non-payment of harbour dues and the 'pub' closed. The ship left the port the following year.

One of the smaller pubs on South Quay was the White Swan, seen here in the 1920s when Daniel Dyson was landlord. On the left is the shop of Seaman the hairdresser. The White Swan was damaged during the war years and was demolished in 1950.

The Upper Ferry Inn in 1903 when William Gedge was landlord. A poster in the window advertises a play at the Royal Aquarium with Lily Langtry as one of the stars. The Upper Ferry, which closed in 1941, had earlier been known as the Yarmouth Arms and the Three Herring. In the doorway is Mrs Gedge with her mother-in-law, whose husband, another William Gedge, was landlord of the Britannia in South Market Road.

The First & Last Tavern, South Quay, was just inside the old medieval town wall and this was a common name for any pub close to a town or village boundary. In 1772 it was known as the Dolphin and later the Ship on the Stocks, reflecting the nearby shipbuilding yards.

The Quay in 1958 when the First & Last was still open. Beyond the pub is Drury House, a fine Elizabethan building demolished in 1969 despite strong opposition by conservationists. The First & Last was demolished in 1989 after being closed for several years.

Left: The South Star, earlier known as the Shipwrights Arms, was demolished after war damage and rebuilt by Lacon's in 1953. In 2002 it was refurbished and became the Quayside Tavern. It stands on land that was at one time part of the fourteenth century Blackfriars monastery.

Below: The Dolphin was built as the Fishwharf Refreshment Rooms to serve the needs of the fish workers in the nineteenth century. It was damaged by a bomb from a Zeppelin in 1915 during one of the first air attacks on this country. After being closed for several years the Dolphin reopened in 1997.

YARMOUTH

four

Beside
the Sea

At either end of the Marine Parade are the North and South Denes. The North Denes is now a holiday site and the South Denes has been given over to industrial and port use. Until the twentieth century, the South Denes was a large area of open ground used only by local fishermen to dry their nets, summer encampments by militia and volunteer soldiers and as a storage area during the autumn herring fishing season. A racecourse had been laid out here and from 1810 regular meetings were held until the course was moved to its present position on the North Denes in 1920. Nelson's Monument, or the Norfolk Pillar, was erected in the centre of the racecourse in 1819 as a monument to the local hero Admiral Lord Nelson and a few years later the keeper of the monument, John Sharman, became the landlord of Monument House, later renamed the Nelson Hotel. Near the harbour mouth a fort had been built in 1653 and by 1819 Paget's Brewery had established a small pub here, known as the Fort, a name later changed to the Ship (see map on page 124) and then Jacob's Boat.

The first Marine Parade was laid out in 1857 between Kimberly Terrace and Britannia Terrace. New buildings soon appeared along the western side, many of them large hotels and public houses. In 1877 the Parade was widened and extended, gardens being laid out on the eastern side. In recent years some licensed premises such as the Royal Alfred, Steam Packet and Norfolk Hotel have been converted into amusement arcades. One of the oldest buildings on the Marine Parade today is the Marine Tavern, a pub which in the eighteenth century was known as the Admiral Onslow, a name taken from one of the Admirals who fought in the battle of Camperdown. The Barking Smack is another long-established pub, at one time playing an important part in the local fishing industry. When fish catches were landed on the beach and auctioned near the jetty, the fish salesmen occupied rooms at the Barking Smack as offices. Mixed in with these older pubs are now many modern bars with names such as Boston's, Mission and Long Bar, designed to cater for the summer holiday trade.

At the north end of the Parade the open Denes now form a large caravan and holiday park. The only pub here, now run as part of the holiday park, is the Iron Duke, first opened in 1940. The name is taken from Admiral Jellicoe's flagship of that name, a ship that fought in the battle of Jutland in 1916.

Right: Nelson's Monument was erected in 1819 with a cottage near the base to house the keeper. This cottage developed into a beerhouse called Monument House, the landlord being John Sharman, also keeper of the monument. The name changed to the Nelson Hotel, seen here. In 1920 a new hotel was built to the east which is today called Winners.

Below: The Gunner, seen here in 1982, opened in February 1938, built by Lacon's on the site of what had been military barracks from 1855 until 1924. In 1996 the pub was refurbished to become the Rok theme bar.

The Victoria Hotel, today the Carlton Hotel, was built in 1841, one of the town's first seaside hotels. It is seen here decorated for the visit of the Prince of Wales in May 1895. There was later a side bar attached to the hotel known as the Bodega Saloon, then Shades and in the 1980s the Penny Farthing.

This Lacon's advertisement appeared in programmes for many of the summer shows in the 1950s and 1960s.

ALWAYS TOP OF THE BILL

LACONS YARMOUTH BEERS

BREWED & BOTTLED BY E. LACON & CO. LTD., GT. YARMOUTH

The Steam Packet, seen here in March 1975, was originally in the building on the right side of the picture that is now the Showboat Amusement Arcade. In the 1970s these two houses were converted into a new Steam Packet, a Steward & Patteson pub. The name changed in the 1980s to the Sandpiper.

In 1991 the Sandpiper closed and was converted into a museum of marine archaeology called Treasureworld. In 1999 this closed and the building is today a Harry Ramsden restaurant. Several pubs along the Marine Parade have been converted to other entertainment centres in recent years.

CHARLES BLAXELL,
STEAM PACKET TAVERN,
South Beach, GREAT YARMOUTH.

This house is situated near the WELLINGTON PIER, and possesses every accommodation, and commanding a beautiful sea view.

CHOICE WINES & SPIRITS!

MEUX AND CO.'S SUPERIOR STOUT AND PORTER.
EVERY ACCOMMODATION FOR VISITORS.

An advertisement dated 1850 for the original Steam Packet. At this date seaside holidays were just beginning and much of the Marine Parade undeveloped, most people visiting the seaside more for health reasons than enjoyment.

Another early seaside hotel was the Royal, opened in 1842 and seen here in the 1880s. Charles Dickens stayed at the Royal for a few days in January 1849 and while in the town he collected material for his book David Copperfield, much of which is based on Yarmouth.

The Marine Tavern is one of the oldest buildings on the Marine Parade, at one time known as the Admiral Onslow. Some of Nelson's sailors are said to have drunk at the Admiral Onslow. In 1820 the name changed to the Marine when the landlord was John Denny and it became the headquarters of one of the beach companies, the Denny Company.

For many years oyster stalls were a feature of the Marine Parade and as early as the 1880s there was an oyster and shellfish stall on the forecourt of the Marine Tavern.

The nineteenth-century beach companies, of which there were seven on the Yarmouth beach, nearly all used pubs as their headquarters. Each company had a lookout, the Denny lookout seen here beside the Marine Hotel. These companies, or groups of men, made a living from salvage from wrecks off the coast.

On the corner with St Peter's Road is the Barking Smack, which until 1845 was called Jacob's Well. At this time the address was simply 'opposite the jetty'. In the nineteenth century, when fish were landed at the jetty and auctioned on the beach, the Barking Smack was used by the fish salesmen who had offices in rooms above the public bar.

The name Barking Smack refers to the fishing smacks of the Hewett Short Blue Fleet which moved from Barking to Gorleston in 1854. In this picture dated March 1987, the pub has become a free house but built into the walls can be seen the Lacon's plaques that still exist on many pubs in the town today.

As their brewery was in a seaside town, Lacon's used a nautical theme in many of their advertisements.

The Bath Hotel was built on the site of the bath house, an eighteenth-century building where visitors could bathe in seawater for medicinal reasons. 'Taking the waters', as this practice was known, became the foundation of the seaside holiday. In this 1899 view, the public bar is on the St Peter's Road end of the building.

By 1987 the whole ground floor had become the Circus Tavern, with the Juggler's Bar at the southern end, names which reflect the proximity of the Hippodrome Circus. Today the ground floor of this building is the Flamingo Amusement Arcade.

The Norfolk Hotel with its public bar in Lancaster Road was established in the mid-nineteenth century. In 1977 the name changed to the Dickens and when the hotel closed it became Boobs, then Cheers and today Boston's. This postcard is dated 1906. Today the bar is a restaurant.

A picture taken in more elegant days when the Norfolk Hotel had its own stables and visitors could hire 'first class Landaus, Broughams, Dog Carts and Wagonnetes'.

The Royal Standard, on the corner of Standard Road, decorated for the 1934 Carnival. Note the 'Jockey Scales' weighing machine on the right. In 1970 the pub was renamed the Crows Nest but today it is the Mint Amusement Arcade.

On the corner of Trafalgar Road was the Holkham Hotel, home of yet another beach company, the Holkham Company. Lacon's bought the building in 1873 and the following year rebuilt it. It is seen here in 1909 with the glass barrel that hung over the entrance, a barrel said to have come from the Crystal Palace Exhibition of 1851. The Holkham closed in 1999 and is to be demolished.

The first Britannia Pier was built in 1858 and a few years later a public bar, known as Uncle Tom's Cabin, was opened under the south side of the pier, the entrance being from the beach. In 1900 the whole pier was demolished, including the Cabin.

The new Britannia Pier opened in 1901 with a large pavilion at the seaward end. In the pavilion was the Balcony Refreshment Room, seen here in June 1902. This pavilion was completely destroyed by fire in 1909. In 1967 a new entrance to the pier was built which now includes a bar called the Pier Tavern.

Elaborately painted signboards are rapidly becoming a thing of the past. Lacon's, like most large brewers, employed their own signwriter to produce these works of art. The origin of the pub signboard dates back to the days when few people could read but a picture could easily be understood.

MARKET TAVERN

Few pubs in the town now have a signboard in the old style. One of the best examples to be seen today is this board on the Market Tavern in the Market Place.

five

Nelson Road

The area of the town between the town walls and the seafront was developed mainly during the period 1835 to 1870. Later development at the northern end took place in the early 1900s, while Newtown developed in the late 1920s. In this area there have been sixty-eight pubs, of which thirty are still open. Many road names and pub names relate to events and people prominent in Nelson's day, the Crimean War or during the reign of Queen Victoria. Nelson Road is the longest road in the town and many pubs are to be found along here, mainly on the corners with the east-west roads. The pubs with 'royal' names include the present Prince Regent, Prince Consort and Alexandra while from the Crimean War comes the Malakoff Tower and the now closed Alma Tavern. Sir Henry Havelock, an English soldier who became a hero during the Indian Mutiny of the 1850s, gave his name to a road as well as the Havelock Tavern (closed in 1914). Another connection with the same historic event was the Lucknow in St Peters Road, the siege of Lucknow having taken place in 1857.

At the southern end of this area of the town were the Victoria Pleasure Gardens. These gardens, an important part of Victorian social life, were opened in 1855 to 'outshine all other gardens'. The south entrance was beside the Clarence Tavern in Clarence Road and at the northern end was the Victoria Gardens pub, which survived until 1998. The gardens, which closed in 1872, were host to many well-known entertainers of the day. One of these was the tightrope walker Blondin, who had crossed Niagara Falls on a tightrope some years earlier and appeared at the Victoria Gardens in 1862. Balloon ascents were popular, the balloons being inflated with gas from the local gasworks. After the closure of the gardens the land was used for housing and Boreham Road built on the site. On Boreham Road was the Gardeners Arms, described in 1896 as 'situated in a good district with lodgings and fish houses around, well built with ten bedrooms'.

In the centre of this area of the town was the silk factory of Grout & Co. Ltd, established on the northern side of St Nicholas Road in 1815, now the site of Sainsbury's supermarket. Opposite the factory gates was the Silk Mills Tavern which, when the factory closed in 1972, took on a more modern name of the Pinball Wizard. Close to the main factory gate was the Factory Tavern, changed today to the Tudor Tavern.

The Bure Hotel on Caister Road, seen here in March 1977, was opened in December 1939 and closed in 1985. Built on the bank of the River Bure by Steward & Patteson, it was next to the factory of Smith's Crisps. The site was later used for housing.

The Admiral Seymour was built in 1888 to serve the needs of the new houses then being built in that part of the town, Salisbury Road, Beaconsfield Road and the many interconnecting roads. This picture was taken in 1905 when Alfred Thomas was landlord.

The Golfers Arms on North Denes Road was built in 1904. The name was taken from the nearby Gt Yarmouth Golf Club on the North Denes. As the housing developments moved north so did the golf club, which in 1913 amalgamated with the Caister club.

An outing preparing to leave the Earl Beaconsfield on the corner of Beaconsfield Road in the 1890s, when William Knights was the landlord. The Earl of Beaconsfield was a title given to the Prime Minister and close friend of the queen, Benjamin Disraeli, in 1876.

Above: Two pubs on triangular sites. The Canterbury Tavern, Middle Market Road, which closed as a pub in 1914 and later became a boarding house and restaurant, and on the right the Peace & Plenty which closed in October 1972 and was demolished when Temple Road was built.

Left: The Hercules Tavern has, since October 2001 been called Drifters. In 1975 it was named the Oliver Twist. This small pub was owned by Lacon's and is the only pub in North Market Road.

Above: In Nelson Road is the Elephant & Castle. On the opposite side of the road was Beach Railway Station from 1877 until 1959, now the coach station. No doubt this pub attracted a lot of trade from railway passengers, particularly during the busy summer months.

Right: The Mitre Tavern was a small beerhouse in St Nicholas Road, closed in 1929 when Nelson Shipp was landlord. Today the site is a car park adjacent to the old town wall.

Opposite above: The Aquarium Hotel, Nelson Road, was originally known as the Northumberland Arms but renamed soon after the nearby Aquarium (now the Hollywood Cinema) opened in 1876. The building was completely destroyed by a direct hit during the bombing of 1941.

Opposite below: William Millington was landlord from 1892 until 1896 during which time he advertised his 'champion dinner'.

The Garibaldi was originally a small beerhouse that was rebuilt in 1888 as a large hotel, which catered for all-male holidays. As many as 6,000 men stayed at the Garibaldi during the season, and were renowned for their high spirits and rowdy behaviour around the town. It 1957 it was rebuilt and the top floors removed. Today it is a nightclub.

A mixed group outside the Garibaldi in the 1930s. Maurice William Drewery Rainer was one of the partners who ran the hotel from 1927 until 1935 following the death of the founder Joseph Powell in 1926. This group is probably dressed for the 1934 Carnival.

The dining hall in the Garibaldi, *c.* 1910. The menu board lists roast duck, roast lamb, rice pudding and tapioca pudding among the daily choice.

The Silk Mills, on the south side of St Nicholas Road, changed to the Pinball Wizard after the closure of the nearby silk factory of Grout & Co. In 2001 the pub finally closed and became a takeaway. This picture of the Silk Mills was taken in January 1975.

The Tanners Arms in Union Road closed in April 1937. Fred Brooks had been landlord since 1908. In the 1860s it had been known as the Farmers Arms but changed after Simon Cobb's tanneries opened in Middle Market Road in the 1880s.

Towards the eastern end of South Market Road was the Britannia, the lease of which was bought by Lacon's in 1903. The Britannia closed in August 1941 and has for many years been a Greek café.

The Wellington Hotel in St Peter's Road is today called the Duke of Wellington. Robert Flaxman was landlord from 1912 until 1927. Before 1870 it was known as the Old Waterloo Tavern.

On the corner of St George's Road was the Anchor & Hope, seen here in 1930. This was a Lacon's pub that closed in 1935 and was demolished in the 1950s. The site became a Dodgem track and by the 1960s it was the Circus Zoo. The Hippodrome building can be seen on the right.

Above: The Rifle Volunteer in Deneside was a small one-room pub run for forty-six years by Walter Bugg. It closed in 1956 when he retired and today is a private house. The Rifle Volunteers had been formed in 1859 and the nearby Drill Hall in York Road was built for them in 1867.

Left: The New Royal Standard in St Peter's Road was from 1983 until 2000 called Sinatra's, but after a short period of closure it reopened in 2002 with its original name.

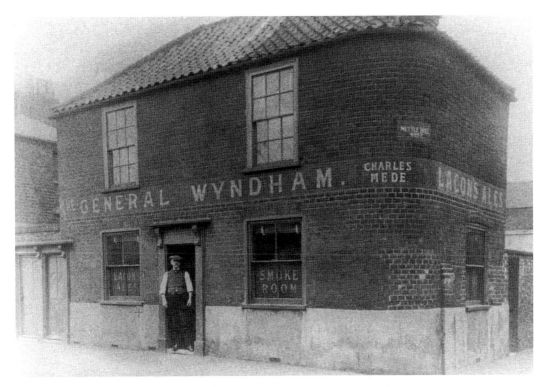

In Nettle Hill West was the General Wyndham, a small Lacon's beerhouse that closed in 1958. Charles Mede was landlord from 1920 until 1933. The name is taken from the family who lived at Felbrigg Hall near Cromer, General Wyndham having risen to prominence during the Crimean War.

Outside the General Wyndham when John Robert was landlord, between 1903 and 1913.

Left: On the west side of Havelock Road was the Crystal Palace, a pretentious name for one of the smallest beerhouses in the town. It closed in 1940 and the site has now been redeveloped.

Below: The Gardeners Arms was in Boreham Road, a road parallel to Havelock Road and built on the site of the Victoria Pleasure Gardens. John Mann was landlord from 1907 until 1935.

The Recruiting Sergeant, a Steward & Patteson pub in Alma Road, is today called the Recruit. This picture was taken in June 1901 when the pub was also a grocer's shop and Louisa Wade made and sold her well-known Dudely Wade's Toffee from the shop. The poster on the wall advertises a comedy at the Royal Aquarium entitled *A Trip to Chinatown*. In the nineteenth century many regiments would station a recruiting team in the town for a short time; in December 1857 the 9th Regiment of Foot visited the town, leaving the following February with 200 new recruits.

In Ordnance Road was a pub called the Ropemakers Arms that closed in 1939 and became an off-licence, the Ordnance Stores, seen here in the 1960s. There were several ropemakers and twine-spinners in this part of the town in the nineteenth century.

The Queens Arms in Queens Road was built in the 1860s. In the 1930s it was the headquarters of the Great Yarmouth Model Yacht Club, seen here with their yachts. This was a popular hobby, the yachts being sailed in the Nelson Gardens boating lake next to the Wellington Pier Gardens.

The Bricklayers Arms on the corner of Victoria Road. When this picture was taken smoking was still an acceptable practice and most pubs had their 'Smoke Rooms'. There is also a separate door for the 'Outdoor Dept' or off sales, a trade that has today been lost to supermarkets.

On the corner of Albion Road is the Great Eastern, seen here in 1912 when it was the only pub in the town to be owned by Fordham's Brewery from the small village of Ashwell in Cambridgeshire. Fordham's later sold the pub to Steward & Patteson.

The Malakhoff Tower formed part of the defences of Sebastapol, the siege of which in 1853 was a major campaign in the Crimean War. This pub in Nelson Road is one of several in the town with names linked to the Crimean War.

Another pub outing by horse transport around the turn of the twentieth century, this one from the Malakhoff Tower. Destination unknown.

Above: In Blackfriars Road was the Floating Light, on the corner with Charles Street. This Lacon's beerhouse opened, *c.* 1869 and closed in 1924. A floating light was the name given to the lightships, provided by Trinity House, to mark safe passages through the treacherous sandbanks off this part of the coast.

Right: The Alexandra in Victoria Road was opened in 1865. In 2001 the bar was renamed Diggers after the landlord Dave Carter, who had been a gravedigger for several years.

Above: At the junction of Camden Road and Blackfriars Road was a pub called the Army and Navy. This closed in 1937 and became a post office for several years. On the right can be seen the Blackfriars Tavern.

Right: The Blackfriars Tavern today has a tiled panel above the door depicting a Black or Dominican Friar, an order who established a church in this part of the town in 1271. The pub was built in 1869 and Hannah Eastick was licensee from 1914 until 1927. Women could only hold a licence if married, her husband probably having been enlisted for war service.

Above: A Steward & Patteson dray outside the shop of Gregory Gedge in Friars Lane in the 1930s. Gedge was a harness-maker who had probably repaired or made the harness seen on these horses.

Left: In Friars Lane this was the original Clipper Schooner, a beerhouse where Thomas Lake was landlord from 1912 until 1923. In 1938 the building was completely rebuilt by Lacon's.

The battle of Camperdown, where the Dutch fleet was defeated, took place in 1799. Admiral Duncan returned to Yarmouth after the battle with eight Dutch ships as prizes. This small pub on the corner of Havelock Place closed in 1937 and is now a private house.

The Columbia Tavern in Apsley Road was bought by Lacon's in 1895. The name is taken from the Columbia fishing fleet that began operating from the port in 1884 and had offices nearby. Herbert Ellis was proprietor from 1896 until 1920 and the vehicle seen here, registration EX6, is said to have been the first motor vehicle to take passengers along the Marine Parade.

Royal Victoria Gardens, Yarmouth.

LICENSED VICTUALLERS

Grand Fete and Gala!

On THURSDAY, 2nd July, 1868, under the immediate
PATRONAGE of

Messrs. Steward and Patteson, I. B. and H. Morgan,

Thornton and Co. | Bullard and Sons
George and Co. | R. Ferrier
Hoare and Co., &c., &c.

Fashionable Entertainment!

Two Performances, 2.30 and 7.30.

☞ Tickets taken up to Wednesday, July 1st, 6d. Admission on the
day, 1s. *SEE POSTERS.*

The Victoria Pleasure Gardens opened in 1855 and closed in 1872. They were the venue for many social events and entertainment including this Grand Fête for the Licensed Victuallers.

When the Pleasure Gardens closed the land was used for housing and the only building to remain was the pub, which had been in the south-west corner. This picture was taken in January 1975 and the pub was demolished in 1998, new houses being built on the site.

Left: The Clarence Tavern, Clarence Road, was built in 1855, part of it being the Albert Gate entrance to the Victoria Gardens. The buildings were demolished in 1972.

Below: The Alma Tavern, 95 Albion Road, closed in 1970 and is now a private house. Another pub with a connection to the Crimean War, it was damaged in the Second World War but remained open, its boarded-up windows having the chalked message, 'This blasted pub is still open'.

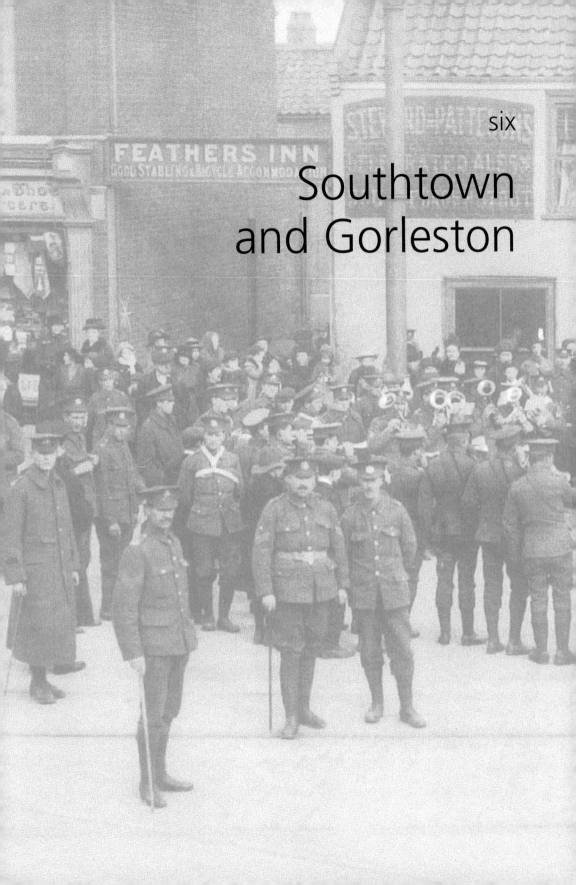

six

Southtown
and Gorleston

On the western side of the river lay the areas of Cobholm, Southtown (at one time called Little Yarmouth) and Gorleston. Cobholm was originally an island separated from Southtown by the Lady Haven stream. Until the nineteenth century this was an important salt-producing area, but by the 1850s the salt industry had finished and Cobholm was developed as an area of housing. There have been only three pubs on Cobholm Island, the Lady Haven and Cobholm Tavern that are still open and the Breydon Arms in Tyrolean Square, which closed in 1968.

Southtown covers an area of about 700 acres and was united with Great Yarmouth in 1668. In the eighteenth century the Anson family, one of who was later to become the Earl of Lichfield, owned the land. In the nineteenth century Southtown became 'an agreeable suburb of Yarmouth' when many businessmen and merchants built their private residences along the main Turnpike Road. In 1887 the Lichfield estate was built on the marshland to the west and to serve the estate two pubs, the Gordon Arms and Lichfield Arms, were opened. The oldest pub in Southtown today is the Rumbold Arms, named after Charles Rumbold, a Member of Parliament for the town nine times in the nineteenth century. A railway station opened in Southtown in 1859 and the Railway Hotel, today the Rocket, was built nearby. Until 1891 the river was the county boundary, Southtown and Gorleston until that time being in Suffolk.

For most of the nineteenth century Gorleston remained a small fishing and farming village on the high ground overlooking the mouth of the River Yare. It was not until post-war development began, to provide new housing to replace that lost in Gt Yarmouth, that Gorleston expanded to the west and more than doubled in size. As would be expected, the old part of Gorleston has many pubs, the oldest to survive today being the Feathers. The small triangular plain that exists in front of the Feathers was at one time the market, complete with Market Cross and pump. Until 1903 the largest fishing fleet in the world operated from Gorleston, the Hewett Short Blue Fleet, and this is remembered today by two pubs, the Short Blue in the High Street and the nearby Dock Tavern. The new post-war housing estates were built on land originally owned by Sir John Fastolfe and later Magdalen College Oxford, and the pubs included in their development – such as the Magdalen Arms, the Cap & Gown and the Fastolfe Arms – all have names linked to this. Beer was brewed in Gorleston for many years at Bells Brewery on the corner of Baker Street and Pier Plain (see map on page 124), a brewery that also owned several pubs in the area. This had earlier been Killett's Brewery. Another small Gorleston brewery was that of George Kew in the High Street, in business from 1876 until 1893. There have been forty-two pubs in Gorleston over the years and today twenty-three are still open.

The Cobholm Tavern, when William Powell was landlord. This dates the picture to some time between 1904 and 1912. In 1922 this pub made the headlines when a young servant girl who lived there took her own life. It was reported as 'The Cobholm Sensation'.

A Lacon's dray outside the Cobholm Tavern in the 1940s when Richard Turrell was landlord. By the 1950s the horse drays had been replaced with motor vehicles.

Above: The Lady Haven takes its name from the stream which at one time separated Cobholm from Southtown, making it an island. Joseph Collins was landlord from 1896 until 1909. Note the tin Congregational Mission Hall next door. The pub was rebuilt in 1956.

Left: The smallest pub in Cobholm was the Breydon Arms in Tyrolean Square, built in the 1860s. This was known to locals as the Garping Gull and closed in 1968.

Above: The Two Bears stands on the corner of Mill Road but when this picture was taken, before 1879, it was the Bear, built soon after the opening of the Southtown Railway Station in 1859. Part of the Two Bears was demolished in 1910 to widen Mill Road (then known as Love Lane).

Right: The East Suffolk Tavern has a name referring to the East Suffolk Regiment that had a depot in the town. The building was refronted in 1911 and in recent years has also been known as Cropper Bar. It is seen here when Louisa Gray was the owner of the free house, between 1903 and 1910.

Opposite above: In Sefton Lane was the Sefton Arms, built *c.* 1854. The pub closed in 1940 but did not reopen after the war. The name was taken from the Earl of Sefton, one of the nineteenth-century trustees of the Lichfield estates.

Opposite below: Southtown Road in the floods of January 1905. On the right is the Anson Arms, the original building having been erected by Samuel Paget the brewer in 1814 on land leased from the Anson family. Commodore George Anson had purchased the land of Southtown in 1734.

Left: In Steam Mill Lane was the New Bridge Tavern, a Lacon's beerhouse that was named after the new Haven Bridge of 1854. It closed in 1928.

Below: The Station Beer Stores, referring to the nearby Southtown Station, opened *c.* 1900. The station closed in 1970 and four years later the pub changed its name to the Rising Flame, a name referring to the offshore oil and gas industry.

The Anson Arms in the 1950s when Fred Leach was landlord. The pub closed in 1958 and the name and licence was transferred to a building on the opposite side of the road, the present Anson Arms. This building is now called Imsco House.

The Half Way House was the halfway point of the Southtown to Gorleston horse tramway which started in 1875. A horse tram can be seen on the right of the picture. Before that it had been known as the Guardian Angel.

The Half Way House closed in 1968, when this picture was taken. It was demolished in 1970 and today houses stand on the site near the Beccles Road High Road junction.

The Southtown maltings of Watney, Combe & Read. The original malting was built by Whitbread's in the seventeenth century. In 1977 the quayside area was sold and demolished but malting continued on the remainder of the site until 1981.

Left: The Belle Vue Tavern on Quay Road, Gorleston was built in 1876. Thomas Overbury was landlord from 1896 until 1910 and the 'late E. Luff' refers to the previous landlord, one Ebenezer Luff.

Below: On the corner of England's Lane and Nelson Road was the England's Hero, a collection of road and pub names in praise of Nelson. The beerhouse closed in March 1967. Bert Houghton was landlord from 1948 until 1961.

The Suffolk Tavern on Pier Plain, seen here in April 1977, changed its name the following year to the Entertainer and in 1982 to the New Entertainer. This was one of the pubs owned by the Gorleston brewery of Bells.

The Waterside Tavern was in Riverside Road. John Hewson, the landlord, is seen here in 1891. In 1903 a factory which turned fish waste into fertiliser was built next door to the pub. This Lacon's beerhouse was destroyed by a direct bomb hit on 19 August 1941.

The Tramway Hotel was built in 1875, on the site of an older pub called the Horse & Groom, the same year the Gorleston Horse Tramway opened. This building was completely destroyed by bombs in June 1941 and the present pub built on the site in 1957.

Opposite below: There have been many pubs in the High Street over the years. The George & Dragon closed in 1925. It was originally one of the pubs owned by Bells Brewery but was taken over by Lacon's in 1865. The site of the George & Dragon is today a car sales area.

Left: Another High Street pub was the Old Commodore. The building seen here was rebuilt in 1935 and in the 1980s was painted pink and renamed the Pink Flamingo. By 1996 it had reverted to the Old Commodore but after refurbishment in 2003 it is now the New Commodore.

Below: The Feathers is probably the oldest surviving pub in Gorleston today. Originally a Bells pub, it was bought by Steward & Patteson in 1845 and refronted in 1870. Charles Dickens is said to have stayed here. Here the 5th Norfolk Regiment is recruiting outside the Feathers in 1914.

On the corner of Pier Plain and Baker Street was the Crown & Anchor, also known for a short time as the Salvage Boat. The poster in the window is advertising a dance at the Floral Hall (now the Ocean Rooms) so the date is probably the 1950s. The name was changed to Cosies in the 1970s and it closed as a pub in 1985, now being a restaurant called Cozies.

The Anchor & Hope was a favourite pub with the beachmen and fishermen of Gorleston throughout the nineteenth century. In 1893 the present Pier Hotel was built on the site of this old beerhouse.

A 1910 Gorleston Lifeboatmen's outing from the Ship on the corner of Pier Walk. A tram can be seen rounding the corner on its way to Brush Quay. In December 1988 the pub was renamed Peggoty's.

At the junction of Beccles Road and High Road was the Greyhound, a Lacon's pub that closed in 1972 and was converted into a private house.

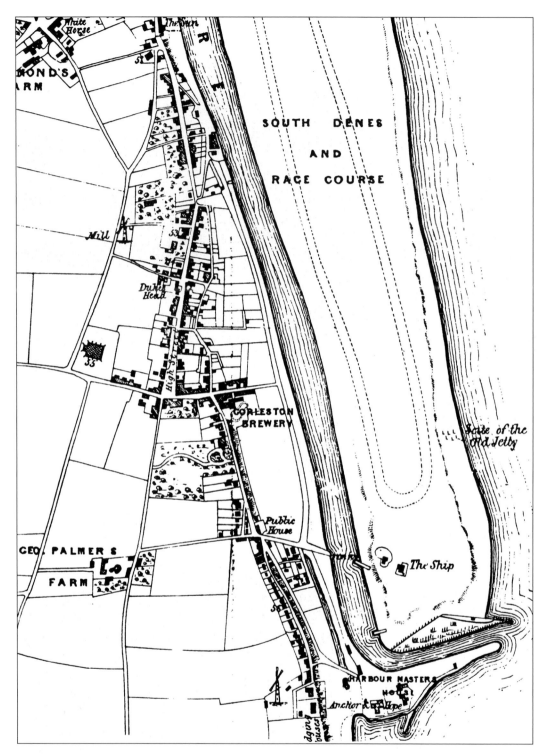

This map is dated 1846 and shows the small fishing village of Gorleston as it was in the mid-nineteenth century. It also shows the site of the Gorleston brewery.

Above: Cliff Hill was the home to many beachmen and the site of a gun platform during the Napoleonic Wars. The original White Lion was rebuilt in 1897 and in 1880 was the headquarters of the Quoit Club, whose season began each year with an onion and lettuce tea followed by a concert. At the foot of the steps is Duncan's Well, sunk to provide fresh water for the fleet during the Napoleonic Wars.

Right: At the junction of Beccles Road and Church Road is the White Horse, originally another pub belonging to Bells Brewery.

The Links Hotel, on Marine Parade, opened in April 1939. This was a Lacon's pub taking its name from the nearby links golf course. It closed in 1998 and was demolished the same year.

The Highlands on Beccles Road opened in 1948. It closed in 1984 following an unfortunate incident that resulted in the death of the landlord. This picture was taken in March 1977. Today the building houses a veterinary hospital.

Index of Pubs

Please note that the letter G refers to Gorleston where there are two pubs with the same name.

Other local titles published by Tempus

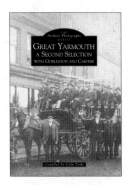

Great Yarmouth: A Second Selection
COLIN TOOKE

This collection of over 200 old images traces some of the changes that have taken place in and around Great Yarmouth and the nearby communities of Gorleston and Caister over the last century. Of special interest to many will be the photographs recording the devastating effects on the area of wartime bombing and also the disastrous East Coast floods of 1953.
0 7524 0643 4

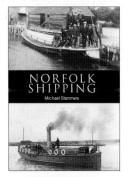

Norfolk Shipping
MICHAEL STAMMERS

The late eighteenth century saw the growth of steam ships and the gradual decline of traditional sailing craft. Norfolk has, though, been a haven for craft such as the fishing vessels that once used the harbour at Great Yarmouth. *Norfolk Shipping* is illustrated with 200 images of just some of the craft that have plied both the North Sea off the coast and inland to the Broads and along the county's main rivers.
0 7524 2757 1

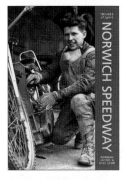

Norwich Speedway
NORMAN JACOBS

Norwich has been one of the most famous and best-loved teams in the history of speedway. From the early days in the 1930s, through the remarkably successful '50s and up to the closure of the promotion in the '60s, this remarkable pictorial history brings the city's rich speedway heritage to life.
0 7524 3152 8

Speedway in East Anglia
NORMAN JACOBS

Containing 200 illustrations, this volume covers the history of speedway in the region from its beginnings on the grass track at the First Stadium in Norwich in 1930 up to the present day. It also features histories of all the local teams including Norwich, Ipswich, Yarmouth, King's Lynn, Rayleigh, Peterborough and Mildenhall, and describes the many star riders associated with East Anglia, including Bert Spencer, Aub Lawson and Ove Fundin.
0 7524 1882 3

If you are interested in purchasing other books published by Tempus, or in case you have difficulty finding any Tempus books in your local bookshop, you can also place orders directly through our website

www.tempus-publishing.com